FOILED AGAIN

WRITTEN BY **MARCIA VAUGHAN** ILLUSTRATED BY **DEREK BRAZELL**

Rigby

You may wonder why a cool guy like me, Robby Gates, is sitting in a fishpond laughing. I wasn't supposed to be sitting in a fishpond. I was supposed to be working with Tiffany Ann Archer on our science fair project. But things didn't go exactly as I'd planned . . .

It started after school. My mom was still at work and my dad was mending the fence behind the barn. That left me to babysit my little sister Sarah. Sarah's OK for a four-year-old, but she's always bugging me to play with her.

Today at 4:00 P.M. Tiffany Ann Archer, the nicest girl in fourth grade, was coming to *my* house. We were assigned to be partners on a science fair project.

I could hardly wait. My only problem was Sarah. She was pestering me already. Tiffany would think I was really strange if she caught me playing silly baby games with a little kid like Sarah.

"Wobby, play with me," Sarah begged as she pulled on my arm.

"I'll play with you now if you leave me alone when Tiffany comes over. We have to work without being bugged. OK?"

"OK, Wobby."

"Do you want to color, Sarah?"

"No. I want to play outer-space chase. You be an alien, Wobby, and I'll chase you away."

"OK. Better run, 'cause here I come," I said.

Sarah shook her head. "No, you got to look like a real *scary* alien."

I sighed. "OK, Sarah. You take some pillows and blankets and turn the couch into your spaceship. I'll dress up and be right back."

I raced to the kitchen. I had to hurry. Outer-space chase had to finish before Tiffany arrived in half an hour. I grabbed a box of aluminum foil, a roll of tape, two spatulas, and a meat baster.

"My alien outfit is going to be great,"
I thought, as I closed the bathroom
door behind me. I started wrapping
foil around my arms, legs, and body,
and reinforced it with strips of tape.

Next I taped a spatula to each ear as antennas. I was definitely looking very cool. Now for the final touch.

I snapped a neon yellow swim cap on my head and pulled a pair of red goggles over my eyes. Wow! I looked really awesome. Sarah was really going to love this!

"Wobby, are you weady yet?" Sarah called from the living room. "My spaceship is landing."

"Fee, fi, foh, fot. I want to catch an astronaut," I called in a deep, robot-like voice. "Better run, 'cause here I come!"

I heard Sarah squeal with delight.

I tried to run down the hall, but the foil above my left knee ripped. I had to walk stiff-legged, like some sort of space monster.

Waving the meat baster like a laser sword, I tromped down the hall into the living room. "Fee, fi, foh, fot—" I began to chant, but I was cut off by Sarah's shrill scream. Her face went as pale as the moon, and her lower lip began to tremble. Tears rolled down her face. She was terrified.

"Where's Wobby? I want Wobby!" she cried.

Before I could explain, she bolted out the front door.

Wobble trot. Wobble trot. I hobbled after her, but she was out of sight.

I searched the bushes beside the porch. I looked around the fishpond. Where was she? I began to worry. What if I couldn't find her? What if she'd really run away from home? How was I going to explain that to Mom and Dad?

Maybe she was hiding in the barn. I doubted that. Sarah was afraid of Gobbler, the turkey. I didn't care much for him either. That cranky old bird would just as soon peck your hand as eat the food in it. I stayed as far away from him as I could.

Wobble trot. Wobble trot. My foil skin sparkled like diamonds in the sunlight as I shuffled down the path to the barn. The door was ajar. I stepped inside.

"Sarah? Are you in here?" I asked as my eyes adjusted to the dim light.

Suddenly I heard a squeak. It reminded me of a rusty hinge. Then Sarah's voice burst from the shadows. "Get him, Gobbler. Get the alien!"

"Sarah, no!" I cried as she swung open the gate to Gobbler's pen.

Gobbler took one look at me and decided I was trouble. He came at me, wings flapping, beak snapping.

"Help! Help!" I screamed and waddled out the barn door as fast as my foil-covered legs could go.

Wobble trot. Wobble trot.

Gobble peck. Gobble peck.

Gobbler overtook me, and he was mad. His sharp beak pecked at the foil on my ankles and legs, cutting it to strips. It peeled off like sunburned skin.

Wobble trot. Wobble trot. I ran faster.

Gobble peck. Gobble peck. The turkey pecked faster, stripping the foil off my backside.

I could feel the cool air on my exposed skin.

I dashed up the steps to the front door and grabbed the knob. Once I got the door open, I'd be safe. I twisted the knob.

It was locked!

I dived behind the bushes, but Gobbler could see the foil sparkling in the sunlight.

Gobble peck. Gobble peck. The noisy turkey ran all around me. I waved the meat baster at him. It just made him madder.

I had only one hope for survival. The fishpond! I hoped turkeys couldn't swim.

Leaping to my feet, I yelled like a madman and charged around the corner of the house, crashing into Tiffany Ann Archer.

"Robby," she grinned, "what are you doing?"

It was a good question, but before I could answer, Gobbler came flying around the corner.

I sidestepped Tiffany and dove antennas-first into the fishpond.

SPLASH!

Gobbler flapped his wings in frustration, pecked the ground twice, then trotted back toward the barn.

Sarah ran around the corner of the house. "Wobby, did the awful alien push you into the pond? Don't worry. I made Gobbler chase him away!"

I sighed and pulled the goggles off my head. "Sarah, there was no alien. It was *me* wrapped up in foil."

Tiffany began to giggle and laugh. I knew she was going to make fun of me for playing such a silly game.

Sarah's eyes grew big. She grinned. "That was fun. Let's do it again, Wobby."

Tiffany looked at Sarah. "Your big brother's really . . ."

I knew she was going to say *strange*. But she didn't.

"Your brother's really a great guy to dress up like an alien for you! Next time I'd like to play, too!"

Then Tiffany Ann Archer looked at me and smiled.

I started to laugh. Even though I was sitting in a slimy fishpond with spatulas taped to my ears, it was one of the best moments of my life.

And until someone brings me a towel, I'm going to stay right here in the fishpond and enjoy it!